practicing to walk
LIKE A HERON

poems by
JACK RIDL

WAYNE STATE UNIVERSITY PRESS   DETROIT

17 16 15 14   5 4 3 2

Library of Congress Cataloging-in-Publication Data
Ridl, Jack.
Practicing to walk like a heron : poems / by Jack Ridl.
p. cm. — (Made in Michigan writers series)
Includes bibliographical references.
ISBN 978-0-8143-3453-9 (pbk. : alk. paper) —
ISBN 978-0-8143-3539-0 (ebook)
I. Title.
PS3568.I3593P73 2013
811'.54--dc23
2012027175

Publication of this book was made possible by a generous gift from
The Meijer Foundation.

Designed and typeset by Maya Whelan
Composed in Chaparral Pro and Frugal Sans

For Vivian and Bruce
For Julie and Meridith
For my mother, father, and sister
And for John Bartley

Contents

3. THE HIDDEN PERMUTATIONS OF SORROW

Acknowledgments

I thank the editors of the following journals for publishing many of these poems, some in different forms:

Alligator Juniper, Artful Dodge, Basilica Review, Big City Lit, Cairn, Chariton Review, Colorado Review, Controlled Burn, Crab Orchard Review, Dogwood, The Driftwood Review, Dunes Review, Eclipse, 5AM, Free Lunch, Harpur Palate, I-70 Review, The Listening Eye, Louisville Review, Michigan Quarterly, Mid-America Review, Nashville Review, National Wetlands Journal, Natural Bridge, North American Review, Pebble Lake Review, Peninsula Writers Anthology, Plainspoke, Poetry East, Prairie Schooner, Rattle, Sou'wester, Sycamore Review, Talking River Review, Temenos, Toad, Water-Stone Review

The poems "Hands" and "The Reunion" were featured on *The Writer's Almanac.*

The group of circus poems was published as a chapbook titled *Outside the Center Ring* (Pudding House Press).

"Easter, 1948" was awarded the Gary Gildner Award for Poetry from the *I-70 Review.*

Thanks to Myra Kohsel and Sarah Baar for their generous help in preparing many of these poems.

Thanks to daughter Meridith for creating the art on the cover. And thanks to the wonders at Wayne State University Press—Maya Whelan, Carrie Downes Teefey, Emily Nowak, Lindsey Alexander, Sarah Murphy. Without your work and support and joy, this collection would never have come into being.

Deep thanks to Jane Bach and Greg Rappleye, who helped every one of these poems.

And gratitude over and over again to Annie Martin, who believed in the work.

My heart's deepest thanks to all of you who have helped these poems along their way. My hope is that you know who you are and that you know how grateful I am.

"Write to Your Unknown Friends"
—*Jeff Gundy*

This is for Bob. He's a good guy, likes
to fly fish, records each catch, where
he caught it, the weather, type of fly,
time of day. He tosses everything back.

This is for Tanya. She's a single mom
with three kids. She works behind
the counter in the post office, knows
everyone in town. Years ago she
threw away the "Return to Sender.
Address Unknown" stamp.

This is for Ted. Ted sells cars.
He wishes cars with fins would
come back. He knows gas mileage
matters. But "You don't see
mileage when a car drives by."

This is for Kenny. He never made it
past the sixth grade. In the winter,
he plows driveways, shovels walks.
The rest of the year he paints houses,
mows lawns, hauls junk. Each morning
he buys a paper, reads it over a cup
of coffee, black, and does the crossword.

This is for Ann. In her backyard, she
has a perennial garden, best in town,
more than a hundred different plants.
She has four greyhounds and a parakeet.
Wherever she goes, she wears a hat.

This is for Martha. She talks to
sparrows. She tries to tell them
something they've never heard.

This is for Sammy. He's always late.
He loves to play blackjack. He's
no good at counting cards. He wants
to own a motorcycle and ride it
to places he's never been—Toledo,
Jacksonville, Los Angeles, Maine.

Today there's no one around.
Too bad. It's a good day
to call some friends, see if
they'd like to come over, shoot
the breeze, have some pizza, maybe
watch an old movie on TV.

Part 1

From Our House to Your House

It's Hard to Know Where to Begin

I could start under a tree outside
my grandmother's kitchen window,
or I could wait until the dog needs
a walk, or I could start over here
by the couch and stack of books.
Maybe not; maybe upstairs under
the bed or even in the basement,
back behind that pile of toys we
keep saying we'll give away.
The garden is a possibility,
around the comfrey or the spent
peonies. Or maybe just here,
where an old man from when
I was a kid came up and asked
if I would look at his hands.

It is 1959. It is the cusp of the coming revolution.
We still like Ike. We are still afraid of Sputnik.
We read *Life* magazine and *Sports Illustrated*
where the athletes grow up shooting hoops
in the driveway, playing catch in the backyard.
We sit on our sectional sofa. My mother loves
Danish modern. Our pants have cuffs. Our hair
is short. We are smiling and we mean it. I am
a guard. My father is my coach. I am sitting
next to him on the bench. I am ready to go in.
My sister will cheer. My mother will make
the pre-game meal from *The Joy of Cooking*.
Buster is a good dog. We are all at an angle.
We are a family at an angle. Our clothes are
pressed. We look into the eye of the camera.
"Look 'em in the eye," my father teaches us.
All we see ahead are wins, good grades,
Christmas. We believe in being happy. We
believe in mowing the lawn, a two-car garage,
a freezer, and what the teacher says. There is
nothing on the wall. We are facing away
from the wall. The jungle is far from home.
Hoses are for cleaning the car, watering
the gardens. My sister walks to school. My
father and I lean into the camera. My mother
and sister sit up straight. Ike has kept us
safe. In the spring, we will have a new car,
a Plymouth Fury with whitewalls and a vinyl top.

From our house
To your house

Season's Greetings

THE RIDLS

In the summer, the pickup
games start by nine or ten

in the park or the field
behind Mrs. Wilson's.

They go all day. Someone's
chosen last every time, stands

in right. The beat-up trucks
start moving around six

in the morning. Jim Miller
spends his day in his "dime store."

At Max's the morning papers
are sold out by nine, but

the coffee's hot and stronger by the hour.
If it's winter, the walks are all shoveled.

If sometimes one isn't, by noon someone
will notice and clear the way, tap on the front door.

The second time we went to Easter church
was the second time we went to church.
I was four, just turned four a few days
before, and when we walked up the aisle
looking for a pew in the crowded church,
I looked up at Jesus on the cross, turned
to my mother and father, and said, "Is
he back up there on that thing again?"
My parents looked down and said, "Yes,"
and they would explain later. We
found a pew near the front, stepping
past those already seated who nodded
and smiled. I could smell perfume and
flowers. Some of the hats were extravagant,
great straw Saturns draped with mesh nets,
and it felt as if the organ's notes weighed
more than the church itself, the great sound
seeming to come from everywhere: down
from the chandeliers, through the stained
glass windows, up from the marble floor.
There was little conversation, a few wisps
of "lovely," "beautiful morning," "Oh yes,
I agree." I kept staring at Jesus. He seemed
to be avoiding my gaze. He seemed to be
pinned there, not exactly like the butterflies
I'd pinched off the blossoms in our garden
and fastened to the black mat I'd bought
at the hobby shop, not exactly like that,
but not unlike that either. How did they
know what he looked like? I wanted
to ask, but the minister stood and then
everyone stood and everyone understood

what to do and bowed their heads and then
raised their heads and we sang and the song
wandered through my ears and into my blood
and I felt I was going to rise off the floor, hover
over the congregation, open my arms to gather
in their voices and the sound of the organ,
float up to Jesus, lift his head, look at his face,
and pull the pins from his huge hands, his bent feet.

Hands

My grandfather grew up holding rags,
pounding his fist into the pocket
of a ball glove, gripping a plumb line
for his father, who built what anyone
needed. At sixteen, wanting to work on
his own, he lied about his age
and for forty-nine years carried his lunch
to the assembly line, where he stood
tightening bolts on air brake after
air brake along the monotonous belt.
Once I asked him how he did that
all those years. He said, "It was only
eight hours a day." Then he closed
his fists. Every night after dinner
and a Pilsner, he worked some more.
In the summer, he'd turn the clay,
grow tomatoes, turnips, peas,
and potatoes behind borders
of bluebells and English daisies.
To keep away the deer and rabbits,
he surrounded it all with marigolds.
When the weather turned to frost,
he went down to the basement,
where until the seeds arrived in March,
he made perfect picture frames, each
glistening with layers of sweet shellac.
His hands were never bored. Even within
his last years, arthritis locked in every
knuckle, he sat in the kitchen carving
wooden houses you could set on a shelf,
each house a little bit different from the others.

Ridl Was Once Spelled Hridl

Bohemian draft runs
from the barrels of Pilzen

to the gnarled streets
of Prague where

Nazis spit
then rolled over

anything left behind.
Here my father

cleared the rubble
and searched

for something
to take home.

Today puppets—
tramps, fiddlers,

clowns, and ballerinas—
dangle and dance

their way along
the ancient stone

bridge carrying
each gray day into

the lingering song of sparrows.

A Midsummer Night's Dream

In my little town, there's a grocery store,
Gilliland's Market. If you are a few dollars
short, "You can bring the rest in next time."

Billy Small, that's his real name, has coffee
at the one restaurant every morning. He's
62, has lived here all his life. They often
ask him to sweep the sidewalks. He
goes all over town, sweeps and smiles.

Brad Pitt and Angelina Jolie do not live
in my little town. But everyone in town
knows them. They try to do some good.

This morning another suicide bomber
killed more than fifty people at a mosque
in Baghdad. They didn't say on the news
how many more than fifty.

In my little town, there are five churches.
There is a park with a playground and
a swimming pool. Kids ride their bikes
and leave them leaning against a tree.

In my little town, there's a garden club.
They meet, talk mostly about perennials.
They keep the town square in bloom and
trim the grass around the memorial to
those from town who died in any war.

My little town's not perfect. There was
a murder/suicide in 1957. The library
needs books. There's no movie theater.
But Mr. Hover will sharpen your mower,
knives, and saws for free. And the butcher
at Gilliland's Market knows the cuts you like.

My Father Was in Love with Peggy Lee

I imagine her purring
her song to him. I imagine
him exhausted, smiling as
her coffee-coated voice
settled into his laboring heart.

The ancients lived between the stars
and the narrow walkways they found
on their earth. That's how it was.

Now when the circus travels at night,
the old clown never knows the name
of the next town. The tent is ragged
by July, the crowd goes home
with the taste of leftover popcorn,
the elephants sway in the morning's dust.

"Is that all there is?" Peggy sang, her face
flat with resignation. My father thought
there was more. He went outside every
day. He washed the car.

Snow clouds hang in the gray air
like bitter metaphysicians. Geese
fly over unzipping the sky.

There was a time before necessity
when the songs were sung in 4/4 time.

Peggy sang to my father all his life.
What did he hear? A long afternoon,
monks in his garden, someone saying yes?

Why did he love her? Her face as indifferent
as ice, her eyes blank as cobalt. Her hair
pulled back flat from her forehead as
severe and tight as the notes she stretched
along that same smoky, perfect pitch.

Her songs sat in her heart like burnt-out
factory workers. Maybe that's what
he knew. Maybe it was the dust
in her voice. Maybe he was dancing.

Open to the Psalms

for Dale Kushner

When you write to us, "Snow coming on the mountains,"
your words arrive as chill and comfort, our nerves now
still with any news, age wandering through us like the quiet

of our blood. We think of you there cabin-sheltered. We
will wait. A week or two. The beeches, maples, willows,
birches, and oaks along the creek now leaf-lost or yellow.

When our time comes to look into our own first snow, I
will think of what I think of every time—how within each
winter's long surround of cold, my father kept the family Bible

on the kitchen table always open to the Psalms. On any morning
I woke early in the iced arrival of the light I would see him turn
a page, slap on his hat, and walk outside to shovel on into the day.

The Steps of Pittsburgh
for my father (1920–95)

After my mother parked the car
at the foot of Cardiac Hill, she
and my sister climbed the steps
to the hospital where my father fell.
The surgeon called to say they
could keep him breathing or
pull the tubes. I said pull them. I
wanted him farther away. Today

a thrush is building a nest in the vines
outside my window. It carries a leaf into
the snarl of branches, sets and steadies it.

712 sets of steps wander up and down
the rolling city. To walk them all, you
would have to lift and set your feet
44,645 times. My father grew up on
Goat Shit Hill. His father carried a lunch
to the mill. After his shift, he and his son

went out back to the hoop on the hill.
My grandfather fed my father hard passes
he had to catch and shoot. A wild miss
would send the ball down the long trail of
twilight disappearing into the valley. This
was my father's way out into the flat world.

Now joggers run the routes of their bluff-top
condos, devise time to stay in shape. My
father's steps got you where you had to go—
up, down, back up to the top of a hill.

It wasn't the way
the old man living
down the street said
he could make it rain.
And it wasn't the widow
who lived in the woods
behind our house who
went for a month without
eating just to cure her
dog of mange. It was
simply the way the town
moved, going from one
small store to the next
before it buried the dead,
or left for good, or held
a picnic. Folklore never
came here. We had cats
and the wind blew hardest
under a full moon, and
young Sam Little drank
the water from Wilson's Pond
and lost his sight, and said
he'd slept with his cousin's
ghost. We still got what we
needed at Miller's Variety Store
and Ken's Grocery. Nearly
all of us went to church.
And Mondays stayed
the same for everyone
except the two brothers
who lived north of the park.

The weather has been in the forties,
certain flowers still holding blooms
as if on real good pot: tea roses hanging
in the light, begonias holding
to their burgundy and white,
coleus stepping out from the melting
ice like little topiary chameleons. I
could use something in my own
heart, maybe some unassuming
jester sitting there, glad and full
of jingles. When things turn
unseasonable, no matter what
the season, I start making
plans to drive north without
a map, wearing a stocking cap
with a moose on it, stopping at
a four-story, one-star hotel where
an eighty-year-old pianist plays
all night in a ten-table lounge.

On My Parents' Sixty-fifth Wedding Anniversary

He would be in his gardens,
picking lettuce, pulling radishes,
deadheading dying flower blossoms.
I know she is still asleep. It's raining,
an all-day rain. You can tell. I listen

to the drops falling on and through
the leaves as I sit here on the porch,
coffee cooling, radio on, books
on the floor beside the daybed,
my grandmother's daybed, the one

I pretended was a crosstown bus.
I drove the brick streets of Pittsburgh
listening for the ring of the bell
when Mrs. Schnelker pulled the cord,
announcing her stop at the corner
of Marshall and Wisteria. "Thank you,"
she'd say stepping cautiously to the curb

where Mr. Westin waited. "Good morning,
"Mr. Westin." "Good morning, Anne."
"Good morning, Mr. Westin," I'd say
when he dropped his coins into the slots
of the fare holder. "Same stop, thank you,"
he'd say. "Yes, Sir," I'd say, the compressed
air whooshing when I closed the door
and cautiously pulled the bus back into traffic.

An Afternoon Visiting My Mother in Assisted Living

You likely know these hallways: doors closed,
small nameplates next to each door, a cluster
of dried flowers on some of the doors. You

can hear the TV behind each door: the news,
a game show, a soap opera, only once in a while
the shopping channel. The air in the halls seems

to sit, piled up on the carpet. You walk through it,
you feel it's been breathed in and breathed out day
in and day out, recycled through lungs that had run

the bases, walked the dogs, pushed generations
of strollers, shopped aisles, climbed stairs to bed.
My mother always laughs when I walk up. She waves.

Out by Petey Bird the parakeet, a half-dozen women
sit on sofas, one doing a crossword, the others
overlapping their small words. Petey Bird hops down

his little yellow ladder and pecks at his image
in the blue-framed mirror hanging halfway up
his cage. "Pretty bird!" he chirps, and I say back,

"Pretty bird!" "Who are you?" two of the women ask.
"Betty's son," I say. "She hit me," one says, "but
she's funny." "We like her," says another and pulls

the shoulder of her dress back up over her bra strap.
"Yes, she is funny all right," I say. In my mother's
room I sit on my mother's bed. She sits in her chair.

We look at old photos she keeps in a flimsy box
in the drawer in the table by her bed. "Nineteen twenty-one," she says.
"These are from 1921. Imagine. I didn't think they had

photos in 1921. This is my dad." She hands me each photo.
"The names are on the back," she says. "Good thing," she
says. "Here's your cousin Dixon with your Uncle Raymond."

She laughs. "I remember them," I say. "You do?" she says.
"I do," I say. "Nineteen twenty-one," she says. And she laughs. She laughs
after she shows me each grainy, copper-faded photograph.

She says, "Aunt Lil," says, "Me and my mother. Uncle Alec and
Aunt Sade. Albert on his pony." Says, "Aunt Lil. Aunt Lil. Aunt
Ede. Uncle Willis and his car. Cousin Cos. Aunt Lil. Dad. Me."

She is laughing when the nurse comes in. "This is my son," she
says and laughs. "He's a poet!" The nurse nods to me, says to
my mother, "Do you remember the rest of the joke you started

to tell me yesterday?" "Which one?" my mother says. Says,
"You mean the one about the two nudes who went into a bar?"
"Yes, that's the one." "No," says my mother and laughs.

Can you tell me which part of this poem isn't true?

There's a bit of a rustle, leaves maybe,
the wind lifting them off the dust
for a second or two. Or a deer, startled,

turning back. Overhead, the clouds go by.
Someone raises the sheets, gives them
a shake, and makes the bed, fluffing the pillow

to finish things. You lie back. There
are dogs in your dreams, a garden, a daughter
picking a flower to bring in to you. She's not

supposed to pick the flowers there. No matter.
Everyone's asleep in another room. When you
opened your eyes, the world stopped, looked

your way, went on. It's like that. The cars go by.
Some people give speeches. Some have it all
figured out. The cardinals and sparrows feed

at the seed outside the window. You used to watch
them. You heard their song. When the big band
played "Satin Doll," you were dancing

again, the ballroom floor glistening under
the sparkle of the spinning silver globe,
everything else a long way away.

I think how good it would be
to spend the day in a garden. Now
how to begin? With some ground
of my own, some good dirt.

How much? Half an acre? Too big?
Not big enough? How deep the good
dirt? Two feet? Seven inches? I'd
need to learn. A book? From the

couple next door? Their garden
thrives. I would get to meet
them. How long has it been?
Four years? What to grow? Flowers?

Vegetables? Both? If flowers—
annuals, perennials, a mix? Sun.
Is there enough sun? Too much?
I will watch the light all day.

Should I grow it all from seed?
Buy established plants? I remember
how my father built a cold frame
from old windows, built it out in the far

right corner of the backyard. I see
myself peering through the windows,
their frames peeling paint in chips
I'd sometimes see catching

in the wind. My father knew
exactly when to lift the windows,
gently dig out the sprouts and plant
them in long, straight, fertilized rows.

This week the letter from my mother
is a half-page long, the handwriting
shaking its way across the paper.
She was proud of her penmanship.

Each loop had been perfect, each
word aligned with the next, each T
crossed as if she used a level.
It was her elegance, a dignity

she held between thumb and
forefinger. "Not much to say,"
she writes. "This room is a room.
They will move me to another."

She always writes on Friday.
"Good way to end the week,"
our years connected from there,
upper left corner, to here centered

perfectly. She would fill two pages
with her crisp judgment of a book,
a movie, descriptions of her times
swimming, dancing, going

to hear the "news lady" talk about
the week's events, how she'd done
on the quiz, and what "The Colonel"
had ordered everyone to do: "Feed

the birds! Clean up the leaves
in front of your place! Support
the troops!" Now she writes,
"I'm tired."

My wife is sleeping on the couch.
It's late afternoon. I watch her
breathing, start to count the breaths,
wonder why, stop. The cat dashes

by. Bees hum in the bee balm.
I pour a cup of coffee, steady it
with milk, stir until it turns from
coal to caramel, the steam rising,

the long evening beginning
to spread itself outside the window.
I look across the room, notice
on the shelf our Scrabble game,

think of the tiles, each letter singular,
able to take its place within a word.

Fractals: A Nocturne

Today we woke to the first snowfall of the season.

You know how it is: The flakes fall and after
the dog goes out, comes in, you wipe his paws.
Or you don't.

My wife has to buy a hospital bed for her father.
His nurses called to say when he lies down
he's in too much pain. They need
to increase his dosages of medication. He was
the captain of the lead destroyer heading
to Cuba during the missile crisis. He
and the crew listened to Radio Havana.
Sometimes to Tito Puente. Kennedy
called him to turn back the fleet. Now
he loves watching *M*A*S*H* on DVD.

This is the holiday season. The deer will soon lie in
the drifts outside our bedroom window. They sleep,
lift their heads, then lower them back into sleep.

Last night we put up a Frazier fir. They hold
their needles. We also untangled the strings
of lights. Eight months before I was born, my father,
white army captain of a black company, led his
men through the rubble of Belgium and France.
The year I was born, he was sent to the Philippines.
We are not treated the same as the others, he wrote,
and we are living in a rice paddy. All there is is rain.

Here it is still snowing.

I have looked through the garage, shelves
stacked with engine oil, cans of paint, piles
of rags and gloves and old hats, boxes
of shoes, nails, broken saw blades, clocks.

And in the crab apple tree he planted
in the back left corner of the yard,
in its burst of white blossoms, in
the empty sparrow nest that has sat
for years within the fork of a branch.

Maybe here, I think, across the room,
sleeping in front of the summer-empty
fireplace, or sitting on the mantle looking
toward the closed white kitchen door.

Or here, right here, in this chair, scribbling
across this very notebook, smiling at each
fallen word, thinking *I still don't know why.*

In the basement? Opening the army steamer
trunk, taking out the medals, the captain's
bars, the box of letters, and the pen-and-ink
drawings he found within the rubble of France.

Or under the dining table, where the dog
sleeps, breathing softly, velvet eyelids ready
to rise at the sound of "Walk," ragged toy lion
lying drool-enameled by his dream-twitching nose.

Or maybe in the sigh at the day's end. Maybe
in the last twenty pages of the book I've been

reading for a week. Maybe I passed by him
at the opening of Chapter Four, when I wondered
why the writer, without warning, shifted point of view.

Part 2
The Enormous Mystery of Couples

I

Sometimes when the dogs are asleep,
and the whole world seems quietly
poised between green and brown,
when everything is lascivious with
leaves—the ground, the porch floor,
the holly bushes, even a few last trees—
you can see a glimpse of the way
the clapboard house was set within
this woods, almost see them nailing
the sills under the windows and
carrying in the kindling. The air
sifts across your forehead, and you
look up, hearing the chill jabber
of the chickadees, the quick
scattering of chipmunks, and
in the anonymous distance,
the disappearance of the sound
of children or was it a car? There
is no need for a letter in the mail,
no thought of putting away
the pots of yellowed impatiens.
Just this little time and
perhaps, a little more.

II

Feeling this way in the afternoon.
Not because it's November. The burnished
landscape lends an invitation to sit,
a blanket across the knees that once bent
and knelt to plant a hundred bulbs,

pull a thousand weeds. This month's
brown cold is welcome. Within the calm,
there is no guilty need to do, no frantic
thought that one had better take advantage
of the long day's light. Oh, the dogs still
need their walk. And there are dishes. But
we can listen to the radio, can watch the slow
breathing of the cats, look for this year's
yearlings as they cross the hill behind the house.
Still the world must make space for us
to sit, walk, sleep, give up itself to give us
room. Later this afternoon, after I build
a fire, we'll pull down our book of maps,
imagine our breath is giving something back,
alchemizing oxygen into gratitude even though
we are an inconvenience in the world.

III

The sun beats down
somewhere else
and the moon is lower
than the tops of the trees.
The cats come back from
their prowl and curl up
in front of the back door.
Coming up the street,
the headlights on the night
shift worker's car turn
into his driveway. We
can hear the refrigerator,
the pump in the basement,
the fan in the bedroom

upstairs. If there are
ghosts, they have only
our silence and the last
of the moon's borrowed light.

IV

Light lies on the oriole's nest,
fallen empty in the euonymus.
Strands of lobelia hang over the edges
of the chipped terra-cotta pots
on the back step. There's an old
novel on the kitchen table, one cat
asleep under the hanging basket.
On the porch a watering can
is giving in to rust. The cracked pink
flamingo stands bent on its iron legs.

V

Two days of soft snow lie
under the moon's stolen light.
It's early winter. Now a quiet
accumulation of cold comes
in its slow way. I wait
for stillness, its stay. Why

think of winter in winter?

Maybe to follow my father
through the old grass into
the deer's long walk across the snow.

VI

Sometimes when the snow
is nearly deep enough
to keep us home, we stay
in anyway, carry in kindling,
build a fire, unfold blankets,
and stack the books we open
now and then. Next to us
we set a pot of coffee, add
a log when we must. Wind
passes, whirling little lifts
of snow against the window.
The dogs sleep as if we're gone.
Others have to leave. We know.
The mail will arrive at noon,
the newspaper by evening.
It won't matter as much.
After sleep, there will be ashes
under the grate, a little less
wood to burn, more or not
as much snow. We may
play some Lester Young
and Etta James, let his sax and
her voice smolder in the coals.

VII

How good it is to be in here,
on the couch, the dogs asleep
against the pillows at the ends
as if we are safe in the great
Kingdom of Rain. Death
with its lisping end rhymes
stands under an umbrella.

The rain against the windows
is a language, its assonance
an uninvited solace. Cold
will come again. We can't
move south. We have sweaters.
We depend on a shovel
and the neighbor's plow.
We depend on music, on
knowing we no longer
need to say we love one
another. Love is Emmanuel.
This rain. The leaves.
This music on the radio
is music on the radio.
The dogs sleep with
their names. These leaves,
this music, this rain

On Going with My Wife to Her Doctor

We don't know what's wrong. We've waited
for more than a year to find out what's wrong.
We've waited for five specialists to tell us
what's wrong. We've waited through thigh-length
blood clots, migraines that seem the eternal
twin of sustained electroshock, pains that twist
her stomach into the devil's balloon animal.
Every diagnosis has amounted to nothing
more than *maybe*. Med after med, strung out
and taken daily, a rosary prescribed by priests
with malpractice insurance. Now here we sit
again. I try to read a month-old *Newsweek*.
They call her name. "You wait here." Yes,
here is where I'll wait. No one sits next to
anyone. Now and then a cough hovers
over all of us. Nearly everyone stares.
Now and then a sigh. Behind the counter,
the kempt receptionist welcomes each entrant,
checks date of birth, current address, accepts
the co-pay. It's mid-April. It's still cold.
One specialist proclaimed, "It's likely lupus."
Another, "Let's first work on those headaches."
Another ordered, "We'll set you up for a series
of steroid shots. Can you start tomorrow?"
I look across the room. The TV is tuned to
a health channel. A woman in a bright pink
shirt is smiling and talking about what to eat.
Sitting under the set is a man, unshaven, cuts
across his forehead. He has a cause and a cure.
"In sickness and in health." I am ashamed.
I open the *Newsweek*: "The War in Iraq."
A nurse calls, "John Larson?" The unshaven

man gets up, walks across the room. "How are
you today?" and they disappear down the hall.
I turn a few pages: Brad and Angelina and
their kids. The woman on the TV is talking
about diabetes. The mail carrier comes in,
drops a stack on the counter. "Hi, girls!"
I think, "We will be okay." I think, "Too
many medications. That many cannot work
together." I laugh to myself thinking, "We're
living in a age of side effects. What would
it be like to have an erection lasting four hours?"
I know in mid-June our gardens will be lush,
blossoms surrounded by the comforting hues
of ground covers, grasses, mosses. Maybe she
will be glad for that. A patient sits down next
to me, asks, "Why are you here?" "It's my
wife." "She sick?" "Yes. You?" "Yeah, I'm
sick too. I think it's just what's going around."

I sit here. You sit there. You love
that rumpled afghan. I keep

wearing this sweater. The snow
is melting in mid-December. You

opened the Advent calendar. I
forgot to empty the litter box.

Words gave way years ago. I
write down everything. You

gave up getting to bed on time.
Two will never become one. Two

become legion. At the terminal
Christmas party, we won't find

each other. You, standing by
a painting of a schooner surging

over a storm's wave, hold your drink
just so, nodding, leaning back in a laugh.

I also nod, listening to the long days
in another's anonymous world. At the table

by an orchestration of hors d'oeuvres,
the newly alone fifth-grade teacher reaches

for a cracker, drops a dollop of pâté
onto its center. Two minus one

equals everything else. We will sleep
within the muted infinity of each other.

Here in mid-January, the drifts have hardened after
a slight snow. The snow is heavy.

The cats are asleep on the couch. The dog
is asleep at my feet.

On the radio, Rachmaninoff, the piano
seeming to be chasing its own notes.

Some mail will come today. Some will not.

Our daughter is now a woman in the world.

This sentence is a sentence. This

In the crabapple tree outside the dining room window,
there is a cardinal's nest covered with snow. Under
the tree we buried the ashes of our first dog.

Later, later tonight, I'll finish the vanilla ice cream.

Lately I've been watching reruns of sitcoms.

Magritte's hats, Duchamp's mustaches, Klee's little envelopes.

When I was ten, a circus came to our town. For fifty cents
you could go inside a tent and see a baby in a bottle.

My father left some of his death behind. My
mother doesn't know.

Outside this window, our daughter
is pulling her sled down the street.

Oh I suppose God could be sitting in the sycamore,
a tree my grandmother called "a filthy thing."

And I suppose God could be all around us: between
that sycamore's branches, in the mortar holding

our house's bricks, in the electrons that type this,
within the current of the creek out back. And oh

I suppose you love me when I walk back in, and
when my jaw drops in a long dream. I suppose

the dog is happy and the window actually lets me
look out into our garden where a hummingbird

sits for, oh I suppose, a second or two, dips, then spins
to another blossom while the kingfisher soars just above

the creek, then settles on an overhanging branch, one in which
I suppose the cells are splitting into something we cannot know.

Here in the time between snow
and the bud of the rhododendron,
we watch the robins, look into

the gray, and narrow our view
to the patches of wild grasses
coming green. The pile of ashes

in the fireplace, haphazard sticks
on the paths and gardens, leaves
tangled in the ivy and periwinkle

lie in wait against our will. This
drawing near of renewal, of stems
and blossoms, the hesitant return

of the anarchy of mud and seed
says *not yet* to the blood's crawl.
When the deer along the stream

look back at us, we know again
we have left them. We pull
a blanket over us when we sleep.

As if living in a prayer, we say
amen to the late arrival of red,
the stun of green, the muted yellow

at the end of every twig. We will
lift up our eyes unto the trees hoping
to discover a gnarled nest within

the branches' negative space. And
we will watch for a fox sparrow
rustling in the dead leaves underneath.

Practicing to Walk Like a Heron

My wife is at the computer. The cat
is sleeping across the soft gold cushion

of my chair. Last night there was a frost.
I am practicing to walk like a heron.

It's the walk of solemn monks
progressing to prayer on stilts,

the deliberate cadence of a waltz
in water. I lift my right leg within

the stillness, within the languid
quiet of a creek, slowly, slowly,

slowly set my foot on the dog-haired
carpet, pause, hold a half note, lift

the left, head steady as a bell before
the ringer tugs the rope. On I walk,

the heron's mute way, across the
room, past my wife who glances

up, holds her slender hands
above the keys until I pass.

Some Notes Taken While the Media Try to Come to Terms with the Life and Death of Michael Jackson

The lilies we transplanted last week seem to be
doing well. It's been hot and dry, but they are fine.

My wife's father didn't recognize her
when she visited him yesterday. He
is now refusing to take a shower. "I'm
not interested any more in being wet."

We skipped going to the fireworks on the Fourth.
Played mah-jongg instead, listened to
the explosions. When our daughter was little,
she would say, "I even love the booms."

This summer a friend of mine's son would be twenty-one.

The Farmers' Market is worth going to if only
for the shades of red and yellow. And the hats.

I keep hearing "Chilly Winds." Do you remember it?
"Wish I were a headlight on a westbound train."

Must remember to put out the recycle bin.

Most everything works sometimes.

It's been a very long time since I've seen
a kid with a BB gun. Or a slingshot.

Last night I went to look at the stars.
It was cloudy. But the stars were there.
I thought I saw a deer settling down into
sleep on the other side of the woodpile.

Even when I look at our dog
I'm surrounded by doubt.

Sleep. Four violins. Wind on its way.

With

*The most important word in the world
is with. We are always with.*

—My daughter, age seven

The sun rises over the trees behind our
house, and the dogs want out. Today

it's supposed to snow again. Tonight
we'll have soup, just the two of us

and talk about our month in Italy,
how we wondered if we could live

in all that light. We'll remember
the last time we danced alone.

The wind is moving across
the drifts as the sparrows, juncos,

nuthatches, and chickadees dart into
the feeder dangling above

the three squirrels grabbing what
falls. Yesterday at the little market

just up the street, the owner asked
how things were. I thought of

my grandmother, how she would
walk "up street" every day

to get a "meat cake" and something
for dessert. Maybe this evening,

before we search for a movie
on TV, we'll go for a walk, take

the dogs, feel the wind on our faces.
I'll take out the trash for the morning

pickup, the night sky draping over
our part of it all; the moon now just

a slice. When I come in, the dogs
will want out before they sleep.

I'll wait for them to come back in.
With no one else, we will say good night.

He gets up first, makes
the coffee while she lets
her dreams come to no
end. He feeds the dogs,
two cups for the big one,
one cup for the pup. She
likes coffee with cream.
He is retired. She goes
to work, brings home
the endless stress of
colleagues convinced
that family and the
next-door neighbors
keep them from seeing
the evening stars or the
weekend's clear air. He
will deadhead the flowers,
carry out the dead mole
the cats fought over during
the night, make the bed,
choose between washing
the windows, the clothes,
the car. Now the coffee's
perked, and he carries it
to her in her favorite cup.
She sits up, smiles. He
says he hopes her meeting
goes well. She says she
hopes his day is nice.
The dogs and cats sleep.
He tunes the radio to
the classical station.

She holds the coffee
between her hands.

Christmas, the Execution of Tookie Williams

My father would be baking kolaches.

I've shoveled the snow from the walk to the house.

Returning home. Leaving home. Finding a home.

The line into the soup kitchen is a block long.

Wood on the fire. Eggnog. Christmas scarves on the dogs.

All night the stars.

The oldest ornament we own, a wooden snowman sitting on a red sled, is
seventy-four.

The delivery trucks follow one another up the hill.

We've placed this year's tea blend in the mailbox.

Each day we rearrange the Christmas cards on our windowsills.

There is a wreath on the door.

What family we have left will not be here.

The cold clings in silver webs on the windows.

A woman behind a counter lays a necklace across her open palm.

Sometimes they
go outside, maybe

move a rosebush
to the back yard or

clean a window.
Usually they

simply stand,
under a maple

or in a snowfall.
And this is often

when they see
a nuthatch on its

dizzy route down
a trunk, or

the quick flick
of a chickadee

across the yard
and onto a branch.

They don't do
much. That's for

others. They know
how to take things

for granted, know
what to miss.

Every morning
they make breakfast.

And when the sun
sets, they let it go.

William Blake's Hiccoughs

Today the soot on the chimney sweeps'
faces soaks up what smog-filtered lantern
light glistens within the streets smoldering

with the filth of pots of peat and chestnuts.
Stir the lemon and the sugar into
this tea, says Mrs. William Blake,

or there could be an earthquake in Peru.
William Blake takes a long sip and counts
to ten. His pen lies between his blunt thumb

and gnarled finger like the beggar sleeping
between a smudge pot and a front step on
Wardour Street. *William?* He nods and hiccoughs.

There is an avalanche in the Alps. The donkeys
in the alleys are restless. Flies swarm at the windows.
Paradise blooms. William Blake sets down his pen,

stands at the window watching the cold rain draining
down the glass. She sits with her knitting. She drops
a stitch. He turns to her, then looks back out into the rain.

She says, "Why not?" Says,
"Corn chips, a long walk, maybe
a new dog, a mutt, half beagle or
one-third collie, one that will sit
on our laps when we watch
the worst shows on TV." I think
TV, but know the shows will
turn into another movie or
a report on raising taxes to build
a dam in Idaho. Sixth grade

was not this frightening, but came
close. Mrs. Kendelton held spelling
bees every Friday afternoon. We'd
stand in a line along the blackboard
in the order we finished the last time.
She kept a record. We spelled
antelope, nuclear, satellite, crèche.
Winners got chopsticks. Amy
Witherspoon finished elementary
school with twenty-seven sets. Losers sat
with their knees pressing against
the bottoms of their desks. This

place is filled with winter. Winter
makes you think about your head, keeps
your mind on the road, roof, the dog
being outside. You have to know how
to spell *rock salt, shovel, scarf.*

Just Before He Had Another Panic Attack

The dog was asleep on the upstairs porch,
and the street in front of the house was quiet.
He was thinking about the night before, how
he'd talked to his daughter who is living

in the South of France. They'd talked about art.
They'd talked about Provencal food and being
dismissed. He had set down the novel he was reading;
he was at that place where you look ahead and try to decide

if it's worth going on. He'd poured himself some
ice tea and he'd wondered about tea, and who
thought of lemon and who tasted the first lemon,
and about the glass, about how his wife had always

laughed at him for using this glass every time
and how she'd always say, "How many ice cubes
did you put in?" and he'd say, "Four." It was
around two in the afternoon. It was about an hour

before the mail would come. And that's why
he'd sat down, taken a sip, the same kind
of sip anyone would take on a summer
afternoon, before the mail arrives, a couple

hours after lunch, a few hours before dinner.

He wakes up, pulls
the blanket higher.
In the house's
pre-furnace chill,
his eyes fill
with the dark
of last week.
She is still asleep.
He can feel her
warmth a part
of him, and he wants
to disappear into
her cells. He wants
the oak and maple
leaves to fall
across their breathing,
cover them in muted
yellows, burnt reds.
But there is the day
and what it holds.
He will enter it
soon enough.
For these minutes
he will let her
and the blanket
be the way it is.

Ron Howard's on the Cover of *AARP*

And I'm old. The light through the window
comes from somewhere even older, and
as it lies across this scrap of legal tablet
I wonder what it would say if we still lived

in the days when we listened to a world
where everything spoke: rain, rivers,
the night sky, each leaf, every shadow.
Maybe the light would tell me to walk

into the day, find a place to sit and see
what the wind brings through the trees.
I'm surprised knowing I want to stay
this old. Ron Howard will always be

Opie carrying a fishing pole, happy
to say, "Hey, Pa," "Hi, Aunt Bee."
The worm he pulled from the earth
drags along the river bottom.

Ron Howard is just past halfway to old.
Sometimes sentimental is our way
of holding on. Sometimes it isn't.
After her husband died, my grandmother

bought one of her town's first televisions.
"They're good company," she said when
The Cisco Kid, Video Ranger, Ed Murrow,
Kukla, Fran, and Ollie came to stay.

Ron Howard's on the cover of *AARP*. I'll skip
the article about him and the one on how to
survive in today's economy. I will do
the crossword. The light from this one sun

will last all day. Tomorrow my wife and I
will canoe on the river. We'll let the current
carry us. When we we've floated far enough,
we'll use our cell phone to call Tom, who will

help us hoist the canoe to the car's roof. The three
of us will drive the back road home, night settling
over the fields of winter wheat, maybe a doe and
her yearling standing in the moon-deflected light.

Assume it's in the kitchen,
under the couch, high
in the pine tree out back,
behind the paint cans
in the garage. Don't try
proving your love
is bigger than the Grand
Canyon, the Milky Way,
the urban sprawl of L.A.
Take it for granted. Take it
out with the garbage. Bring
it in with the takeout. Take
it for a walk with the dog.
Wake it every day, say,
"Good morning." Then
make the coffee. Warm
the cups. Don't expect much
of the day. Be glad when
you make it back to bed.
Be glad he threw out that
box of old hats. Be glad
she leaves her shoes
in the hall. Snow will
come. Spring will show up.
Summer will be humid.
The leaves will fall
in the fall. That's more
than you need. We can
love anybody, even
everybody. But *you*
can love the silence,
sighing and saying to

yourself, "That's her."
"That's him." Then to
each other, "I know!
Let's go out for breakfast!"

My Wife Has Sent Me an Email

My wife has sent me an email.
She asks if we have enough coffee

for the weekend. She adds, "I love
you." I hit reply and type, "Yes,

we have plenty, two bags of
French Roast in fact. We'll be

fine." I add, "I love you, too"
and hit send. I am sitting in

our living room, laptop on my
lap. She is sitting in her office

upstairs. We are emailing
in our own home. We have

lived here for thirty-five years. Outside
my window, in the garden, outside

hers, in a window box, June's
early rise of zinnias and salvia

lifts to bloom amid the dusty miller.
It is raining, the rain dousing

the cosmos and cleome as it falls
from the roof. She emails, "You

should see this rain from up here."
I email, "You should see the rain

from down here." Yesterday after
a nice lunch together I got up

and went to the garage and sorted
through the shelves not knowing

what I was looking for. After lunch
today, I'm going to find the trowel

my father used. I'll get a rag and
some rust remover and bring it back.

A Quiet Study in Black and Gray

They watched the Academy Awards
night before last, all those gowns.
Harriet got five of the winners right.
Carl three. "I guess we aren't

movie buffs," said Carl. "No, guess
not." "Remember," Carl said, "when
we went at least four or five times
a month? We had money then." "No

we didn't. We needed a car and a
vacuum cleaner." This morning
they got up, let the dog out, changed
the litter in the cat box. They had

oatmeal. Carl shoveled the walk.
Harriet paid some bills online.
Every morning about a dozen deer
cross the creek behind their house.

Harriet calls Carl to watch. They
stand at the window. She says,
"Don't move. They'll see us."
He puts his hands in his pockets.

You are so beautiful the chickens
are sleeping beside the wheelbarrow.

In fact, you are so beautiful that the chickadees
in the trees, the hemlocks specifically,
are putting aside their seeds.

The logs are burning down
into ashes. We will clean the ashes
from the fireplace in May, carry
them out and spread them on the roses.

How many million galaxies?

You are so beautiful that after the last
of the breakfast dishes are put away,
we will plan our next vacation. Or we won't.

And God said, "

Right now, this very minute, eleven deer are crossing
the stream behind the house. It is ten degrees.
My grandmother lived to be 104. And you are
so beautiful.

Maybe it actually was the plums.

My grandmother was sad. Could be she didn't mind.

On the other hand

When I pray in the morning, I offer the day.

When I pray in the evening, I offer the night.

In the spring then the rain. This morning
the light lacing salmon pink
along the ridge of poplars.

You really are so beautiful.

It's my job to pull the strings
of duck weed from the little pond
that sits along the walk. We hope

those stopping by will pause and
watch for the goldfish we pretend are
koi. And when I wonder why we love

them, I remember it is because
there are days when we are
the fish. With a flick of a fin

we glide under the water irises or rise
for a bit of sunlight dappled on the
surface. We swim, dive, pucker toward

the scrim of shade for pellets of shrimp.
We know nothing of the heron wading
in the stream, the raccoons in the woods.

We are simply rising and diving within the light.

Putting Away the Santas

He has found one for her every summer,
some in Christmas stores that keep things
in a desperate sparkle all year long, some
in antique shops, some at garage sales.
He sets them along the windowsills here
in the house they bought and thought
would be the first in a line leading to
the perfect home. Now they can't leave
the creek that bends its way through
the woods out back. The morning light
slides through the jagged space
between these handmade bedraggles
in divinity. Their beards flow or scraggle
down across their chests, unfurling
from their rust-red cheeks. Some raise
their arms in unabashed glee. Others
are weary, their eyes soft, their hands
barely holding on to a bear or wreath.
A few are tiny, a few are tall. One is
straight as the back of a Swedish chair,
a couple are full of gnarled Appalachian
cuts and curves. One plays the accordion;
one holds back seven dogs. Some look
as if their sacks are full of sorrow.
Their daughter made one from a
toilet paper roll. He puts them out the day
after Thanksgiving, welcomes each one
back, asks how their sleep among
the ornaments has gone, even thanks
them for lasting one more year. Now
he wraps them one by one in a paper towel,

lays each back in its box. Come mid-July
He will start the search again, hoping he can
find another jolly lugger of unaccustomed joy.

Hardship in a Nice Place

The roof on our house slants out
over the garden, and if it rains,
the water falls on what blossoms

still arc in late August. My wife
is sleeping through her day. There
is a breeze here on the porch. There

is a certain slant of light collapsing
through the beech trees on the hill. One
tree fell this afternoon. I could hear it

cracking into the quiet, saw an angle
of trunk begin to lean and rustle
its branches across the limbs along

the stagger of woods. At night, sounds
come that I can never identify. It's often
like that, our long days lacking much

of anything that can be named.
My wife will sleep. I will walk
to the mailbox with our dog.

The best place to be is here,
at home, the two of us, while

others ski or eat out. It will be
quiet. We won't watch the ball

fall, the crowd in Times Square.
They will celebrate while here

there is this night. Tomorrow
some will start over, or vow

to stop something; maybe try
again. Here the snow will

fall through the light over
the back door and gather

on the steps. We will hope
our daughter will be safe.

She will wonder what
the year will bring. Maybe

we will say a prayer.

Have You Heard the One About?

I remember when an exquisitely staged,
mute Buster Keaton pratfall or a lucidly lurid
Mel Brooks non sequitur or one of Jack Benny's

long-and-dry-as-a-desert stares or a Stan to
Ollie, "Well *now* we're getting somewhere"
would light my belly, my mouth widening

with my eyes, the air catching in its open hand
whatever comes from who knows where and
scattering good taste and decorum out of every

niche and nook and cranny from my ear clear
to my ankle. Now I smile. I'm glad I do. There
are days dappled with things that squint my eyes,

that lead to the sweetness of sighing. It can be a last
marigold holding its old frazzle of a bloom into
the first snow, an audacious crocus leaning into the last.

It can be the light of a wide afternoon, or even
the dishes stacked in the sink, sometimes an unmade
bed, always the cat asleep on the warmth of the dryer.

And it still can still be you.

The gods are tired of tending fires.
Against the window, a cold rain.

Each night the hour hand moves
time and us closer to the light.

No one wants to go out. No one
wants to stay in. And the rain.

Robins do their silly walk across the lawn,
dead grass dangling from their beaks.

Crocuses raise their purple risk
through the ice-crusted mulch of maple,

oak, beech, and willow. They last
a day. Clumps of daffodils stay

blossom-tight. We want to put away
sweaters. What would the saints do?

We haul in more wood. It is raining.
Sunday and it is raining. And it is cold.

Winter's wedged itself into a crack
along the equinox. We know, in time,

the trees will bud, the flowers rise
and bloom. We do what the earth does.

I'm working a Sudoku puzzle, one cat
in my lap and Mozart on the radio. I
didn't catch what work, but I don't know

much about classical music. I like it,
most of it, have it on all day, a companion
as I wander from room to room within

a life that may or may not matter. I
also don't know much about cats. We
have two. They act as if they can't believe

the other should be in the house. They hiss,
growl, swat at each other. The old dog
sleeps. The young dog stands between them.

It's a cold day, patches of snow and ice.
There are birds at the feeders. There is
a clear sky, and the creek behind the house

drifts along as does the next piece on the radio,
something by Edward Elgar or maybe it's
Vaughn Williams. This puzzle is impossible.

Interlude

"Hey Skinny, the Circus Is in Town!"

Circus: Late Summer

Everything is fading: the dark blue
canopy of sky over the three rings
is as washed out as an old pair
of jeans, its galaxy of bright
white stars leaning into gray.
The center poles, once varnished
slick as the sideshow barker's pitch,
now match the dust carried in
from the back lot. It's late August.
The elephants sway in the fly-biting
heat, their dusty trunks twisting mats
of hay into their hot mouths. The big
cats sprawl against the bars of their cages,
twitching their tails, staring, panting.
The sequins on every costume
have dimmed, the sparkle
disappearing into the black holes
of two shows a day. Tiaras sit tarnished
on the dry hair of the queens of the air,
high wire, horse's back. The red, orange,
blue, white, silver, gold hyperbole
of the midway, the shrill paint
along the sides of the semis
have turned mute, their audacity of color
as tame as any gentrified downtown.
Even the balloon man's voice has
dropped an octave into a sand-papered
plea, and the ringmaster feels the weariness
in his throat when he brings on "The
Amazing Zambini Brothers Who Will

Thrill You with Pyromaniacal Feats of
Flying Flames!" After the show,
the roustabouts drag the tent
like their own missed chance.
The nights on the cots are hot.
No one is clean.
Two months until winter quarters.
A rain will cool things off and only make it worse.

Outside the Center Ring

It's another night in another town
and one by one the great gray elephants,
the pink tips of their trunks wrapped
around one another's tails, parade
through the main tent's faded entrance.
This morning the roustabouts tightened
the guy lines for the wire-walking Alberto,
steadied the rigging for The Family
of Flying Falleronis. Now outside
the center ring the clowns wait to honk
their trumpet-sized horns, slap each
other's painted faces with mitts the size
of frying pans, the grease-paint caked and
cracked across their eyes. No one will laugh.
Between each act, the roustabouts write home
or sleep while in the next town, the advance man
stakes the lot and heads on, tacking arrows
on telephone poles to mark the way. Straw boss
slides some tens into his pocket, tosses a few
receipts into the green book, pours Jack Daniels
over chips of ice from the mess tent, takes
a sip, heads out to the back lot to wait for
the tear down. The sun's dropped into the end
of the day, the night sky holding to the moon's light
falling over the patched canvas. There's the faint
ripple of thunder. No one can prepare for mud.
Across the lot, behind the power truck, two kids
fumble under each other's clothes,
talk of running away with the show,
having their own act, he spinning her

in the death spiral high above the center ring.
After the sale of prize candy, "a circus souvenir
in every box," the roustabouts move out, start
stacking the empty seats on the flatbeds, and
the elephants rise up on the long line. Then
the disappointed crowd wanders out
into the night and a last chance
to buy a circus program, balloon, cloud
of cotton candy. At the entrance the elephant boy
waits to fasten the chain around the leg of Suzie,
who will walk around the tent, pausing
at each stake as the boy tosses the links up into
the moonlit air, lets the chain drop and loop
as he hollers, "Hunh, Suzie. Hunh!" and she will
slowly lift her leathered foot, the iron rising
from the earth then falling back against the dust.

Grouse of the Circus Boss

They might as well be sitting
on their hands, he says, nodding
toward the audience hunched
on the plank seats surrounding
the three rings. They wouldn't
know death if it knocked,
don't know what it takes to walk
a wire, enter a cage of cats, time
a leap into a catcher's chalky grip,
the mad defiance of it all. They
all want special effects, have
no idea a roustabout in black
waits under the trapeze, lies
beside the tigers' flaming hoop,
softly whistles to the wire walker's
dance. We can't compete
with light shows, surround
sound, wide-screen outer space.
Oh, they'd go to a freak show,
but Four-Armed Arnold,
Seal Girl, and The Human
Blockhead live along the Gulf,
collect unemployment, play
hearts, and trim the bougainvillea
climbing on the fence out front.
We're here to say to hell
with that. Take a chance.
Fly across the center ring. Hang
from the top of the tent by your hair.

After the Lion Tamer

The juggler dances into the center ring,
tosses a red pin toward the top
of the tent, then flings a green one,
then a yellow, one red, one
green, one yellow all tumbling
after one another, he catching,
tossing, catching the red one,
the green one, the yellow one,
the red, the green, the yellow, red,
green, yellow, and then he hops
on a star-covered ball, keeps
the red, green, yellow pins spinning
up to their peak, then down, then
he extends one leg and loops a silver
hoop around his ankle. He stands one-
legged on the spinning ball, the pins
spinning, the hoop spinning, the world
spinning, and then the cymbals crash
and he flips backward off the ball, kicks
the hoop into the air, while each pin falls
fast into his hands, the silver hoop following
down to land around his neck. He bows.
There's a drum roll, a soft swish of cymbals
and scampering through the entrance,
a Chihuahua in a striped and pointed hat.
It jumps onto the juggler's outstretched hand,
stands on its front paws as the juggler elegantly
turns full circle to show the crowd, then
tosses the tiny dog and it lazily arcs its way up

toward the lights then down to land
on his other hand. He grabs an umbrella
from a purple stand and tosses it, the dog
now following the tumbling umbrella.
Then he adds a bright blue derby hat, the three
chasing one another in a hallucinatory
Mobius strip painted by Magritte, all
moving as if there is no wobble in the world.
Suddenly, a pistol shot rings out.
The umbrella drops, its tip sticking
in the sawdust. The juggler leans on it
with sparkling insouciance, extends his hand
like a common dandy and the dog lands.
Then the derby spins down, jauntily settles
on the juggler's head, a bullet hole dead center.

Sequins

Hanging in the silver trailer
her pickup pulls to every lot,

150 costumes sparkle in the light.
She used to watch each act unfold,

told herself one day she'd fly,
dance along the wire, or twirl high

over the center ring clinging
to a spinning rope. Now

she sews: repairs split seams,
stitches galaxies of sequins,

adds lace, fringe, a braided edge
of gold. On her cot, after threading

through another day, she sees
the costumes sparkling on her ceiling,

traces them floating in her sleep.
And every afternoon and night,

they shine under the spotlights
like tiny stars. Sometimes

she puts down her needle and
walks to the tent, stands in

the entrance, and watches her sequins
glisten in the capes of the Flying Alhambras.

Daydreams of the Catcher
of the Queen of the Air

I

He waits for the subtle
nod, feels it in his fingers,
and swings into a triple,
out into the anonymity of air,
his wrists at the last locking
into his catcher's unassuming
grip. He hears the crowd's
inhaled hush, the sighing
exhale, then swings back
and twists, kicks, lands
poised as a pen on the reliable
bar, ready for his insouciant bow.

II

The shag of the lion's mane
glows golden in the center ring,
the great cat's mouth opening
as if yawning into the abyss.
He slowly folds his hands
behind his back and lays his
head on the slab of the tamed
tongue. The cymbals' swish
keeps time with the swish
of the lion's tail, the audience still
as the dusty air until he steps back,
raising his head from the lion's maw.

He then stands in the light's haze
and bows to their anonymous awe.

III

He swirls his cape
within the ring of fire,
pulls a silver sword
from his star-sparkling
scabbard and thrusts it
into the flames. He leans
back, slowly raises the blade,
poses the point in a pirouette
above his fierce face, then
sends the blade down his throat.
Extending his arms, he becomes
a sword himself, and with the panache
of an indifferent dandy he walks around the ring
as if to say he has no need for anyone's applause.

"She's kept me off drugs," her handler
says, standing beside Suzie, waiting
to lead her under the half-risen big top.
She will pull the center pole into place,
lifting the patched and restitched
stretch of sky-blue canvas streaked
with stars toward the clouds hanging
over the lot. Every morning
after the roustabouts, staggering
from bad wine, heat, and three hours'
sleep in the sweat-drenched bunks
stacked five high in the semi
that hauls them from job to job,
have driven the stakes, looped
the guy ropes over the side poles,
and unfolded the unrolled midway
and main tent, after the great hum
of the power generator has been
hooked into the lights that tonight
will glow across the cornfields, Suzie
hears the elephant boy holler, "Hunh,
Suzie, hunh," and feels the quick, dull
thwack of his hook against her side.
She, swaying like a great gray ship
docked in the daylight, lifts
her accustomed trunk and, dust
flying off her back, trots as she has
every workday for forty years
in through the main entrance

and stands where the roustabouts
will later piece together each fading
arc of the red center ring. The handler
hooks the enormous clank of chain
to her leathered harness, again
shouts, "Hunh, Suzie, hunh," and
she, with a slow wave of her crusty
ears, caked and sore from a thousand
bites, walks with the indifference
of sovereignty to the far end
of the tent, pulling the great pole up
and into place, the pole itself carrying
the sky and all its stars from the dust.

The Death of the Queen of the Air

That night, the roustabouts, stacked
four beds high in their semi, slept,
and the lions rolled over in their cages.
She died in her sleep—not a fall
from high above the center ring, not
an overdose. After her bow,
she went back to her silver Airstream,
lay on her purple sheets, and fell
asleep. She had always flown.
Even as a child she'd swung high
above us all. Twice a day she smiled
down on her audience, took a breath,
timed her leap, the bar always feeling
as if it knew her callused and chalky
hands, her catcher waiting rhythmic
for her grasp. At the end of her act,
she defied death with "The Triple,"
whirling in the still air through three
somersaults before grabbing the wrists
of her steady catcher. She dazzled
dangling from his faithful grip.
After one more full swing, she'd spin
a half-turn back to her bar. The time
she nearly missed, her left hand slipped,
the chalk falling like stardust through the lights.
She never forgot glancing down, seeing
her body twisted on the sawdust in the center
of the ring. Death was her rigger, tightening
the guy wires, checking the play in the ropes,

securing each clamp, bolt, and stake.
And Death was a roustabout, waiting,
watching her sparkling sequins, her gold tiara
catching the spotlight, her dark and silken hair
flowing out behind her as she'd swing.
She wore red for the matinee. Silver
for the evening show. And always
the gold tiara as twice a day she flew
through the empty and indifferent air.

Circus Cook

Damn, I love bacon grease. I'd love
to be buried in the stuff. Just spread it
over me—let me smell it into heaven.
Or what the hell, into hell. That'd be
something, me frying in my own grease.
Been with the show thirty years, hardly
ever seen an act. Coffee's always ready,
strong. Complaints? Cut it with milk
or water. They do two shows a day.
Me, three. Hell, I'm center ring
more than the elephants! Every day

I find a grocery willing to sell all
its lettuce, potatoes, butter, beans,
bread, and chicken. Breakfast sits out
all morning. By noon I've spread a lunch
for the roustabouts, sweating and cranky
after raising the big top, tightening
the riggings. Dinner's on the plank tables
by five. No flowers here. No candles. You
want those, *you* bring 'em. Silverware
and dishes steam overnight while the trucks
haul ass for the next small town. I'm up
by 5am. By six I've piled the toast, am
frying eggs. And there's the coffee.

When I was a kid, made all my own meals.
Nothin' fancy then. Nothin' fancy now.
I've got my own restaurant and no competition,

no worries about pullin' in customers. You want
something better, go to town, cook in your
own trailer. I've fried eggs in almost every
state; in the rain, the drought, through
a couple tornadoes, winds that ripped
this canvas off the stakes. Sure sometimes

I wonder about being a real chef, chopping
parsley and tossing croutons on a salad,
coming up with recipes using olive oil.
I think about writing my own cookbook,
Meals for a Center Ring. But I'd have to
figure out portions. And who'd buy a book
four pages long? Monday—breakfast:
toast, coffee, eggs, bacon, hash browns.
Lunch: sandwiches, soup in a kettle, iced tea,
Jell-O. Dinner: hash browns, chicken, beans, bread,
Jell-O. Any leftovers, toss together into "Circus
Surprise." Tuesday through Sunday: Repeat.
Vary amounts depending on number of roustabouts.

After *my* finale, there's no bow. No one applauds.
At each meal, the ringmaster ought to introduce me.
"Ladies and gentlemen, children of all ages, may I
direct your attention to the center chopping block,
to The Amazing Hank, King of the Culinary Arts,
Master Chef of the Midway who will dazzle
your taste buds with his mouth-watering fare,
with his expeditious, exotically delicious,
stupendously resplendent, delectable delicacies
concocted for your savory pleasure before the day

has even dawned, before the stinkin' matinee,
before the god-damned evening's performance,
the ingredients gathered from the deepest, darkest aisles
of your own local Super Value Mart! A drum roll, please!"

The End of the Fat Lady

> Come on down in a little closer and
> let me tell you about some of the
> strange people we have on the inside.
>
> —*Traditional sideshow bark*

She lies back, spreads her arms
and legs, and makes an angel
in the snow, her smile unfolding
into the falling flakes, her eyes
opening into the gray day's sky.
She holds her place on this wintered
earth, wonders if the snow, cold and
soft against her thighs, could ever
deepen enough to bury her. Would
she die before a thaw? Years ago

she sat in the swelter of summer
absorbed in the daily empty gazes
at her anonymous fat. She never
spoke as they walked by. No one
paused. Some glanced back,
caught her eye, and she would stare
into all she knew they thought: Poor
thing. How does she move? What
makes someone gain all that weight?
If she smiled, they would turn away,
head on to gawk at Seal Boy and
The Half Girl. She wanted to tell them,

"No. Down deep I am not the same
as you. Down deep there is just

more fat. And a barge, a team
of tired horses, and a dozen books
I've read a hundred times. Nothing
else." Then the morning after
the sideshow closed for good,
there was only the sky. In winter,
summer, every day, the sky.

Death in the Dog Act

Tonight he placed a bright
red chair in the center ring,
and seven dogs jumped
through hoops, danced
on their hind legs, caught
hats, and carried tiny umbrellas,
lined up behind the star-covered
baby buggy, pushing it around
the ring. One by one they slid
down the silver slide,
then ended the act as they always
have—strutting between his legs
as he nonchalantly strolled
with his silver cane. They
snapped up their cookies
and took a final bow. Now,
back outside his silver trailer,
the dogs lie on their spots,
their heads soft on their paws.
He pours Jim Beam
over ice, takes off his black
tie and tails, walks among them
as he does after every show.
Along a circus's wayward route,
there's no right place
to bury a dog, only the next
town. He reaches down to
scratch each one behind an ear,
their tails wagging in the dust.

The Children of the Lion Tamer

The lion tamer's children sleep
between towns, wake up
in the late morning, never know
where they are. While other kids
let in the cat, feed the dogs, head
to school, the lion tamer's children
carry meat to the great cats lying
in their cages, toss the heavy shanks
between the bars. They watch
the lions, tigers, jaguars yawn,
tear, and gnaw, and then they
return to the family's silver
Airstream, their home within
the hometowns of everyone else.
Hoisting their light beams and
atomic rays, they turn the dust
on the back lot into the ash of Jupiter
and search for nine-armed aliens.
Their father sleeps. Their mother sits
in the morning sun, tries to keep
her eye on the kids while shining
his black leather boots. She wonders
where she is, wishes she knew
what her children will know,
if they'll ever live in winter, have
an after-school job, years under one roof.
She's forgotten what it was like
to watch a car leave a driveway,
have to get along with the strange kid

on the next block, knock on her best
friend's door after a fight. She watches
her children hold back the aliens,
listens as they order the enemy
to turn over their weapons,
take them back to their spacecraft,
show them the fastest way back to Earth.

Roustabout

It's a bed. Can't gripe.
Plenty of coffee. Have
my mug. Been here
with the show ten years.
Once took off to try
some factory work.
Hated it. Every day
was Monday. Always
the same place. Here it's
a new town, something
new to talk about, deal
with—mud, wind, broken
rigging, ripped canvas.

During matinees we bet
on Alfredo, if he'll try
a triple, and every night
after tear down, we see
if the town's got any action.
But you turn on a townie,
you're gone. One guy lost it
in Nebraska somewhere. "No
one pulls a knife on me," he
growled walking off the lot.

Most guys last two, three years.
A few jump mid-July. I can't
settle. Rather be nowhere, be
nobody. Put up the tent,

play some cards, during the show
take a nap, eat, tear down, roll up
the canvas, pull up the stakes.

Clown

Every day he disappears
rubbing the thick, white paint
deep into his web of wrinkles,
down his leathered neck, across
his forehead, watching the old
skin turn into Jocko, interlocutor
of laughs. He lives hidden
behind the diamond eyes,
red glob of a nose, mouth
petrified wide in a grin.
He's glad to lose his face
behind the permanence
of clown. Entering the center
ring, he pushes a piglet
in a wobbly, wicker pram,
stops under the spotlight,
stoops, and slowly steps into
a little red schoolhouse.
The audience quiets, waits,
and when the band strikes up
"Pomp and Circumstance,"
the pig, full-grown in cap and
gown, strolls out, Jocko trailing
on a silver leash. They promenade
once around the ring, then out
and back to the trailer where
Jocko hangs up the leash, sits,
feels the entrance of gratitude
for his red nose and graven smile.

As he scrubs away the whiteface,
red and yellow paint, the silver
stars above each eyebrow, a face
appears, one he doesn't recognize,
one that stares then turns away.

The balloons float red,
blue, green, yellow—planets
swaying in an orbital pause
above his head, a string
their link to gravity, his fist
the center of their universe.
They are for sale. The show
is over, the crowd emptying
out wandering toward him.
Dollar for a plain one, buck fifty
for a clown's face, an elephant
on a stool, or a wire walker.
He barks their need for a last-
chance souvenir as the roustabouts
pull down the poles, and the tent
comes down like a last heaved
breath. Nearly everyone passes
him by. A few fathers succumb.
He looks up into the moon's light
bright above the sawdust and wonders
What is a balloon? What big cat
does it keep from clawing
the whip handle? Suddenly
his sky turns black, clouds
drawing themselves across
the stars. He thinks this
must be how The Great Rollo
felt that night in Cincinnati
when he lost his grip, spinning

into an anarchy of flips,
somersaulting down into
the dust. He sees his fist open,
watches the balloons float
toward the vanishing moon.

Night on the Circus Lot

The big cats sleep.
The drivers, too, each chin
against a chest, knees still bent
and pressed against a dashboard,
their trucks parked between
the stakes that mark where
to unload the riggings, poles,
and canvas when the first light
falls over the lot. Straw boss
makes his rounds, flashlight
beam leading from truck to truck
to camper to the semi where
the roustabouts snore four
high in their bunks. He looks
under each rig, his light raking
the grass for a loose wire, leak,
thief, kid wanting to leave town
hiding behind a tire of a sixteen wheeler.
The night's common quiet
counterpoints the generator's hum,
the steady center of the show."
It's hot, humid, clear,
the stars reliable in their singular space.
He sees a light on in Don Axelia's
Airstream, walks over, waves
his beam across the silver half-shine
of the tightrope walker's home,
sees him sitting at his little foldout table,
turning the pages of the local paper.

Don Axelia looks up, squints, comes
to the door. "Saw your light. Thought
I'd better check. Everyone's in for the night,
even Kenny with his arms around a bottle."
"I'm fine. You were a wire walker.
You know how it is." Straw boss
nods. "I do. Try and get some sleep."
He turns off the flashlight. He knows
his way back through the dark.

Winter Quarters

The circus knows no winter cold,
no drifts of snow across the midway,
the elephants' backs, the semis
that haul the riggings, tents, poles,
props, and cats. Here The Great
Mendoni barbecues a chicken,
Madame Sashay knits a sweater
for her daughter's newborn, and
the Belardo Brothers are fixing
the roof of their light blue stucco
one-story. They all wonder
what it's like along the route, if
the snow's knee-deep in Minnesota,
if the ice is building up in Kansas.
They imagine flakes piled high
as the high wire; sleet freezing
on the trapeze; icicles hanging
from the bridles of the Lippizans,
along the rim of the big cats' cage.
Here it's three months in the sun
with The Flying Garonis searching
for a new trick, Peppo training
a new dog, Miss Lilly revamping
the opening, the anonymous roustabouts
painting the trucks, rings, and props.
The boredom of somersaulting
through the empty air, coaxing
a lazy lion through a flaming hoop,
dancing across a high wire as you

juggle a china vase, Turkish scabbard,
and a Russian doll disappears
like The Amazing Human Ghost.
Everyone's life comes back: buying
groceries, playing a game of hearts
around the kitchen table, weeding
vegetables in the back yard. At night,
when they look up at the moon
crawling across the sky, they think
tomorrow we'll arrive right here.
No next show until March when
the trucks roll off the lot onto the road.

Part 3
The Hidden
Permutations of Sorrow

The Two Chairs in the Garden

The obligatory nap has disappeared
into the light that falls after 4pm.
It is time

for the sweet blue of cornflower,
the muted palette of mums. This
is something I love: the season

between seasons. I feel at home
within this turning, summer's heat
dwindling into the mellow nowhere

of sixty-five degrees. Cold coming. This
space with no particular demand, no
order to cultivate or repair, no wood

to bring in, no seed to plant, no need
to hope. Just here, in a safe hint
of later: cool inhale, the gentle

clatter of acorns on the porch roof,
the chattering argument of squirrels.
There is a certain stillness in this small world,

the light lying across each unshaded
petal, rock, branch, the faded paint flaking
like haiku from the two chairs in the garden.

Trying to know what to do is difficult
enough, let alone knowing what to do

anyway. I could take that at least two ways,
maybe more. For example, I could take a walk,

even a long walk and I would expect to walk
through the woods or a field or a park or downtown.

But what if I didn't take a walk and instead just kept
the walk to myself, kept it here amid all the indecision

about where to take that walk? I might pop open a Coke,
kick off my hiking boots, put on a smoking jacket,

and pile up some Jane Austen and some Henry James,
just pile them up. And then maybe I'd talk with you

even though you are no longer here. It could be like that,
or maybe it is like that. And at night the sky would be full

of the same stars as the night before last. At least it seems that way.

for John Bartley

Within the Moment of Indefinite Suffering

All it takes is a tick. You can be walking
your dog. Your dog can be stopping to
sniff a patch of jewelweed or pausing
to pee on a post surrounded by poison ivy.

You could be watching a swallowtail slowly
lifting and settling its wings while resting on
a swatch of crown vetch. The sun could be
lost behind clouds, clustered in a cumulous

mound of white or sinister gray, the moon
could be full, waning, new, the stars moving
across their scrim of deep space, everything
still benign in its revolving threat. You

could be sweeping the walk, passing under
the pergola draped in wisteria, wedding veil,
honeysuckle, or merely sitting on the bench
beside the brook out back. Or taking a path

through the park, joggers steady-stepping, or
walking along the well-worn trail to the pond
at the edge of town where you could be sitting
under the willow, its branches hanging their braids

over your wait for the sunfish to surface. It could all be
beautiful: the day, the light, the breeze bending the tall grass.

for the victims of the politics of Lyme disease

He thought he would build a fence.
Not to keep anything out or in. He'd
make it of stones and branches
piled in the woods out back. He'd
weave the branches. He'd balance

the stones, make the fence
a mixed reminder, two textures,
one holding him to the ground,
one taking him into what
is above. He would sit by

the window and watch her walk
along it, touching the wood and
stone. She would stop to notice
how he had finely fit each rock
and branch, the wind able to move

through each open place. A sparrow
would come, perch long enough
to open a seed. Squirrels would
run along the ridge. He thought
he would plant English ivy,

burning bush, and wedding veil,
hoping to see them climb, spread,
entangle, bring out the unnamable
hues of green, see them catch
the light and glisten in the rain.

He would bring in firewood, get
a dog. He would make the coffee.

Listening to Chopin in Early Winter

The first snow is falling.
There is no one here.
wisteria branches   On the dining table, I've
twisting gray-brown set the season's candles.

This is not the right time to wonder
where my father is now.
The wind is lifting the dead   beneath the beech tree
branches. They will or will not   the bird's nest

break. I'll sit by the window,
the candles   watch the snow quiet the day, stumble
the bittersweet   into an impossible hope. I want to pray.
The nocturnes are playing. Next

the etudes. Then the ballades.
the evergreens   If I could be these notes.

Yesterday was a death march.
                                    along the stream
There is no longer a word
two deer

for this. There is duration.

At the "As the Spirit Moves" Poetry Reading

Everyone waits for everyone. Everyone
stares at the floor, then up to the ceiling,

then back to the floor. Then a small voice
says, "I'll read," and we listen to how her dog

ran away. She was a little girl, maybe nine, when
her dog ran away, and now her dog is running away

again, is trotting along each line of her poem, stopping
now and then to sniff a post or a pile of leaves, a comma,

sometimes at a caesura, sometimes at the end of a line.
On he goes, away from her, off into the woods or

across the railroad tracks or into town through some
back yards, down an alley, into a garden. She tries

to follow, calling after him. Between each line, she
yells, "Sammy! Here Sammy! Let's go home, Sammy!"

That last "Sammy" stretching out across each syllable.

He'd work the garden until dark,
now and then looking up

to see if she was looking out
the window. She'd loved roses.

After three years, he gave up,
started sleeping on the left side,

and instead of planting roses,
filled the plot with tomatoes,

beans, zucchini, and asparagus.
The next year he added eggplant

then mixed in impatiens, pansies,
obedient plant, asters, autumn joy.

He loved to be surprised by a tomato
showing up within a mass of lobelia,

to discover peas climbing a tangle
of cosmos, lilies, and cleome,

to find a squash under the geraniums.

It was always there to load, carry,
spread in every bed, along the edges
of the paths he'd carved through
the woods that hid his home. He'd

say, "I love knowing every spring
I'll need to haul again." Over the long
snows, last year's mulch, smothered
somewhere back within the fallen

leaves, lost its thick dark brow, leaving
a ghostly gray that in the day gave nothing
back when the light fell into the morning.
There was no getting the tiny clogs of dry

dirt from under his jagged fingernails.
"I'm not going anywhere," he'd smile.
The piles came every April. He'd wait
three days, letting the air settling into

the earth settle into the mulch. "It comes
alive," he'd say. Then on the morning of
the fourth day, he would wake, dress, look
at his nails, have his coffee, and head to the

shed. He'd take down his shovel, push
his wheelbarrow to the pile and begin.
With each shovelful he breathed in the dark
damp then turned and, like the mule he liked

to think he was, pulled his way first to the peonies
where handful after handful he'd lay the worm-

warm mulch around the wine-red stems that rose
every May since his grandfather planted the roots.

What are you doing among the dead? Playing
cards, slipping an ace up your sleeve?

      Angels in the woodshop
      make footstools, bulldog
      doorstops, and toy outhouses
      that explode when you open the door.

This is no place for Renoir. Hopper would have painted the neighbor on the porch.
  Frida, you would be my friend. You would
         have slept on the couch.

Row, row, row, row, row, row, row, row, row
      your own boat.

I am thinking of all the stones in the world.

      "Alone" is an oxymoron.
      How anonymously absurd.

In this hour, there are no hours: the beech tree
   outside the window, the deer asleep
     on the cold grass, a solar
       system, a star.

And the books, Mahler's Fourth, a daughter walking in the garden,
a kingfisher and the turkeys high in the winter branches over the river.

A Man I Know

A man I know walks down the road
behind his house. All year, he wears
a scarf and stocking cap. When he
nears our place, the dogs bark.

I know there is always grape jelly
on his shelf. He told me. And he also
told me at night he thinks about birds.

Sometimes he decides to stop by.
He says he wants to visit the dogs.
They like him. Sometimes he sits
with them at our window and draws.
He loves to draw apples. He also

enjoys the gray squirrel with tan ears
that scrounges in the back yard for
what the juncos, blackcaps, and
sparrows drop from the feeder. He talks
a lot about when he was in third grade.

Why not "It's been a good life.
I sucked out lots of marrow"?

Why not "The cabin was cold,
but I got a book out of it"? Or

how about "Wolf. Settler."
"Honeybee. Loner." Or "Why

all those beans?" Or "My god,
I kept track of everything except

my own pencil!" When my time
comes, I wonder what I'll say.

"I loved you and I'm sorry"?
"I was one surrounded by luck"?

I'll likely lie there, eyes searching
into the air, and chirp, "Chocolate.

Tallahassee." Or "Kitty cat. Real
estate assessor." "Moose. Indian."

Poor Emerson.
He was always so above it all.

Several Old People Are Walking by Our Window

It is snowing. They
used to be children.
In that clump of trees
across the street is where
they would build a fort,
lay in supplies to last
until spring: some bread,
a few oranges, a pack
of Tootsie Rolls. This
snow is supposed to fall
all day. They are wearing
long coats. Their steps
lead them. They smile
as they remember hearing
a parent or a bully saying,
"You better watch your step!"
The tops of their hats lean
into the wind, the blowing
snow something they are
glad to walk against. They
notice the ice left from the
recent thaw, its patches
glistening along the walk.

Dogs live knowing how to live; they defy Kierkegaard.

Lighthouses may well still be useful.

God is likely tired of being God.

If you wait long enough, the shadows . . .

Despite what they say, it can be good to take a nap longer than twenty minutes.

Rain that never falls is still rain.

Amen is the only way out.

Honeysuckle, like love, grows anyway.

Etudes could well be beautiful when played on a kazoo.

The lyricism of early morning often arrives unaccountably.

He Brings Home Everything

Under the house there's room for a cat.
The porch is piled with clocks, bicycles,
broken windows, toasters, magazines.
The kitchen has minarets and steeples and
towers of old tins, cereal boxes, the top
one always with a face: Hopalong Cassidy,
Willie Mays, Daffy Duck. Every shelf
holds a montage of mugs, matchboxes,
old platters, coffee pots, an entanglement
of whisks, forks, ladles, and spoons.

A hornet's nest dangles from the ceiling fan
hanging next to a mobile of fish bones.
The bathtub overflows with children's books.
Four years ago, he closed the door on two
of the bedrooms. In his own room: puppets,
trains, kites, stuffed and wooden animals,
pop-up books, soldiers, clowns, snow
globes, penny banks, tin cars and trucks.
There's a rowboat covering a leak in the roof.

These blues were never in the world.
He would have had to let his palette

find this benign freeze, this landscape
still as a stoic's paradise. The ice must

have lain beneath his frayed gray gloves
as he thrust his brush stiff across

the canvas. His red spreads from the sun.
Nothing else moves. In this infinity

of cold, this pitiless lucidity of fading light,
the dead walk across the river into town.

One wing of a monarch butterfly lying on the back porch steps.

Over the hill, the old goat. . . .

Call me when the X-rays come in. I may
need to find a ride.

Angels, after they have fallen, often love to
    go horseback riding in the rain.

When the house painter goes home after work, he
    goes for a walk with his dog. He
    never takes a leash.

God needs a god.

This long stretch of highway, this grapefruit, this only way
to say it's sad but not that bad.

                    Before the beginning, between
the title and what follows, in there, in that space,
that's where the horses rest.

_____, and _____, or _____, but
_____; whereas,_____, but, then, of course _____

                    Last night.

What goes best with Kant's metaphysics? Would
    it be better

without

a beverage?

Outside, the rain on the roof. Inside, the rain on the roof.

A family of six leaves Ogden, Utah at nine in the morning
traveling east toward Salinas, Ohio. A car
full of thieves leaves Albany, New York at seven
at night heading west toward Saginaw, Michigan.
If the family drives an average of 57 mph

Whenever he fell asleep on the couch,
she would get out her puppets.

Tell the audience the show is about to begin.

Cue the quiet.

Cue the curtain.

Enter Rabbit. He moves slowly across the stage.
Pauses.
Looks out at the audience. Does
a double take. (Wait for laughter.)

"Well! Hi there! You here for the show?"

"Rabbit?" Rabbit looks down. "What?"

"I can't get the anvil up on to the stage."

"You can't get the anvil up on to the stage?"

"No. Can't. Give me a hand, would you?"

Rabbit shakes his head at the audience, looks
down. "Oh my. Yes, it is big, isn't it!"

"Yes. And heavy. Help me with it."

"What will we do with it once we get it up here?"

"We'll juggle it."

"We'll what?"

"We'll juggle it."

"Just it?"

"Well, no, not just it. I have
a few other things to mix in."

"Like what?"

"Well, here, take this feather."

Feather comes up from below.

Rabbit takes it, waves it a bit, sets it down.
"What else?"

"Here. This map of Ohio."

Map comes up. Rabbit sets it beside the feather.
"That it?"

"No. One more thing: this."

"What?"

"This."

"What's this?"

"This."

"I don't see a thing."

"It's last Wednesday. Take it.

138

Careful. It's awkward. You'll
have to pull it."

Rabbit pulls.

"Keep pulling. Good.
There's a lot more of it."

Rabbit pulls some more, says,
"We're going to juggle a feather,
a map of Ohio, last Wednesday,
and an anvil?"

"Right."

"I don't think we can."

"We can."

"I don't think we can."

"We can."

"I don't think so."

"We can. Keep pulling."

"We may need some help."

"Keep pulling. Uh oh."

"What?"

"I can't find the anvil."

"You can't find the anvil."

"Right. I can't find the anvil. It was right here a minute ago. Keep pulling."

Rabbit keeps pulling.

Everything gets quiet.

Rabbit looks around.
"Hey!"

Silence.

"Where's . . ."

Silence.

Rabbit looks at audience.

Curtain.

The last time I saw them we were young.
Ginny was a cheerleader. Ben was getting
A's in trig. Tonight we glance at nametags.
Around the cheese tray, we say, "Of course

I remember you." "Yes, four years ago.
Things are better now." "No, she never
graduated, moved. I don't know where."

We look good. The food is just fine. The music
brings it all back, and we dance the latest steps
across our brain's prom floor. It's all the same.

And nothing is. We're still dumb kids, just gray
and tame. If we had it to do again, we'd get it
right. Some are sure they got it right the first

time. They ask for another Manhattan, dry
martini, scotch on the rocks. They glisten
in their tans. They watch the rest of us,

the ones with comb-overs, two divorces,
the ones who look for lower gas prices,
a good night's sleep, group tours.

The Dogs' Door Is at the Far End of the House

They wake up at the foot of the bed, stretch,
yawn, shake, and take the long walk—through
three rooms, down the stairs, down the hall,
left into the work room, then through their door
into the day's early glaze—to pee. Overnight
there may have been a four-foot fall of snow;
sleet may dagger down like a glass sky
shattered by some exasperated god; an August
huff of humid heat may settle in their fur; they
may slip in the slick mud from a spring or
summer downpour; ticks can drop and stick.
No matter, they go out, pushing their dripping
noses against the cold or heat of the flapping
door, leaving behind the steady hum of furnace
or air conditioner, sniff their way to their
well-marked spot, squat—and pee. Like stoics
matted in hair shirts, they go out, come back
dry, soaked, snow-coated, mud-caked. I
wonder if they wonder what waits
on the other side. They never complain
or balk. They walk, let go, find their
momentary stay against the coming day.
Finished, the young pup prances
to the door, hops through, dashes to his bowl.
The old dog stays out sitting in the morning air.
His great gray head moving slowly back and forth,
he sniffs the center of his universe, his place
in the aromas of the day. Then, nose full, he
limps to the door, lifts each front leg, pulls
his back legs through, and pants his way
back through the waking house to sleep.

The Artist to the Canvas

I see the lost
light of the dead,
the occult of morning,

the same moon
rising behind the night.

The next child is
the next child, each
stillbirth
chasing the disappearing
world.

I let you in the back door,
mortician of beginnings,

tramp
sleeping in a newly mown field.

A Wednesday afternoon with no thought of Thursday

Three weeks in the woods, two by myself, one with my father

My father

Cups of tea, plates of sugar cookies, the first ones I ever made,
the dough still sticking to my fingertips

Comic books from the late '40s: *Little Lulu*, *The Green Hornet*, *Felix the Cat*

Every creek from the upper peninsula of Michigan

The last page from twenty unpublished novels

The ease of a dog's sleep

Five gold rings

A moon-draped evening among the birds in the hemlocks

Any snow-covered pile of leaves

Photographs, I don't care how many, of my daughter just before she smiles
for the camera

Seven moments with the lucidity of cutting yourself with a bread knife

Whatever happens between what happens

The liturgy of an old monk laughing

But He Loved His Dog

Wednesday was trash day so he pulled
the garbage can to the curb. There
was never that much in it. Sometimes
he stood there for a few minutes, looking
down when a car drove by, looking up
at the trees in the yard across the street.

No one really knew if he knew anyone.
He had a dog. It wasn't much of a dog.
It was an old dog, a mix too mixed
to know what all might be there. He
told someone once, "Oh I suppose
there has to be some beagle, maybe
some German shepherd." Each noon
he walked the dog down to the corner,
left on Maple Avenue, three blocks
to the park where they would stop and

he would sit on a bench under a beech tree
that had been hollowing out for years.
The dog lay at his feet, once in a while
lifted its head and sniffed. He never read
or talked except to say, "What do you
think of this day, boy?" and the dog
would wag its tail across the gravel path.

He would sit for most of the afternoon,
then tug on the dog's leash and they
would walk on through the park, then
back home. He would bring in the mail,
toss it away. When the evening's light
began drawing its shadow across his porch,

he would turn on the radio, open a window,
and sit outside, with his dog, listening.

A Cabinet of Natural Curiosities

Love. Our dog, asleep on the comforter
we tossed on the bed just for him.

The sound of the furnace. A fire
in the fireplace. The temperature
outside: twelve degrees. My

mother sleeping in assisted living.
That we are not grandparents. Tonight
on ESPN, number one playing number four.
One will lose.

LED bulbs throughout the house.
Too many books on the shelves.

Early afternoon. Nine recordings
of John Lee Hooker. The rakes
in the garage. The shovels, too.

Cacti along the south windowsill.
The bed. The pillows on the bed.

A collection of mah-jongg tiles. A
Scrabble game. Nothing under
the magnets on the refrigerator.

The drawing our daughter made in third grade.

We watch her, right leg collapsing
with each step, she leaning down,
hobbling onto her knee. Lying
behind the snow-covered
woodpile, the mother, her head
high, her eyes wide, her tail
white-flagging in the flakes.
In this winter—the most snow-filled

in half a century—the deer paw
into the drifts, chew what the books
say deer will never eat. They tear
the leaves from rhododendrons,
shear the grasses along the walk,
pull the ivy down in strings from
the beeches and maples, off the pock-
marked bricks on the south-side wall.

Our cats lie along the windowsill,
watch, tails twitching. Our dog
runs howling through the dog door
out into his acre where he leaps
against the chain links. The deer
look up, but stay. Are they
too hungry to be frightened? We
don't know what to do. We don't

know what to say, something
dumb and sentimental. Does
the yearling know her leg
is shattered? When she lifts
her good leg, the other hoof

gives way in the soft snow,
her knee settling into a drift—
this now her own hideous walk

within the world. Is this a kind
of love we cannot know, the deer
spared our ignorant pity? She
stumbles to another bush, the dog
barking, the cats' tails twitching,
our words dumb, lost without
a sentence to make sense in.

The thing is this rain keeps
falling and the long notion
of another day stays

relentless as a ringing phone.
What if you made up who you are
and why your mother never ate cereal,

why your father was a night watchman
in his own home? You keep things
tidy and full of happy endings. You

rearrange the empty jars in the cellar,
remembering the way you strained
the apricots, blueberries, raspberries,

how you stirred the apple butter, sealed
and labeled each jar. You sort through
the gladiolus bulbs lying on the frayed

window screens, pull off new tubers,
count them to see if you'll have too
many in the summer when the

wheatgrass around your house has grown
so thick the cats can hide. You swipe
the webs from corners of the windows,

go back upstairs, sit down with a drink,
the windows open, and you smile as you tell
yourself the same old jokes your father told.

The knitters sit with their knitting
sitting in their laps, their fingers
nimble as mice feet as their needles

twirl two-color twitches of yarn
into well-reasoned whorls, their
work their letter to the cold world.

Sunlight falls across the silence.
Then, "My daughter is leaving."
Here the house is around them.

In the fields there are horses.
"Do you think she will stay?"
Some spin their own yarn.

The wool matters. "I don't
know." They have time in
their hands. Here language

has no translation. Sheep are
messengers. The snow lies
over their gardens, gardens

that will rise in the late spring.
"I hope she will find something."
They knit together once a week.

They knit alone. They knit
in church, at meetings. They say,
"What are you working on?"

The gods are snoring. The snow,
a sugar snow, falls like a scrim
across the outer world.

         A long
winter's ashes have settled
in the fireplace, miniature gray
dunes. A charred log lies
across the andirons.

           The dogs sleep.
The cats sleep. No
branches move. The air is there,
in a stillness lost on those who
cannot see it matters.

   My mother will sleep most of the day.
   My father will sleep all day.

There is dust on the shelves, along
the top ridge of each book.

On the windowsill, a jar of peppercorns,
half a bottle of brandy.

A walking stick by the door.

I have been reading *The Art of Babar*. Yesterday
I spent some time wondering why. Today I don't.
I look at the spaces between each word.

Time burns. We're out of matches.
We're also out of milk.

For Lenny

After the first of my best friends died,
I sat for a moment
and I listened
and the only sounds were the sounds
that had been there all along.
Dogs know this every day.

I called my wife
to give her a message.
But I didn't tell her.

Our garden had never been this lush
this early in the year.
And our dog was asleep.

Outside, the air was filled
with the songs of cardinals, jays,
and my neighbor's rake.
She was clearing a space
for her lavender, bellflower,
and a plant whose name she forgot.

After the first of my best friends died,
I looked out the window, then
put on an old record, thought
about baking bread, stared
at the painting of my wife and daughter.

On the shelf across the room
was a large beige pottery bowl
and a small beige potter cup.
The light was touching them.

The snow is falling through eternity's quiet
where everything lives within. And now
mid-morning the sunlight falls across the

hemlocks, it too lying within the ubiquity
of quiet, a quiet arriving from the silence
that was here before Alpha and will be here

after Omega. This morning when the turkeys,
twelve of them, tumbled in their tumultuous
flutter down from roosting in the dark

where they sleep one hundred feet up in
the empty-leaved maples, the snow shook
down on the quiet of the cat, and she rushed

through the brush to the back door where she waited
for me. The quiet, of course, was everywhere.
The turkeys nodded their stable way up the hill,

following the inevitable trail that has become
their day, seeming to trust the path will bring
them to seeds and corn, lost fruit. The light

glistened along the sheen of their backs bringing
gold and green out from what against the drifts
seemed only a study in black. Sound does come,

even in the hush of the turkeys' enormous feet
imprinting the snowfall, even in the small fall
of flake upon flake. Quiet can turn to silence.

After Spending the Morning Baking Bread

Our cat lies across the stove's front burners,
right leg hanging over the oven door. He
is looking into the pantry where his bowl
sits full on the counter. His smaller dish,
the one for his splash of cream, sits empty.
Say yes to wanting to be this cat. Say
yes to wanting to lie across the leftover
warmth, letting it rise into your soft belly,
spreading into every twitch of whisker, twist
of fur and cell, through the Mobius strip
of your bloodstream. You won't know
you will die. You won't know the mice
do not exist for you. If a lap is empty and
warm, you will land on it, feel an unsteady
hand along your back, fingers scratching
behind your ear. You will purr.

Return to a Place I Don't Remember

There is no one here again. Next
to the shed where he built cabinets,

a sumac twists its rusty brushes.
The air feels filled with lost smells: mint,

lilac, mud-caked corms, moldering
grass. Weren't there cows here? Fences?

Boulders, a barn, a path the herd
walked to be fed, milked? Wasn't

there a grove of maples near
the pasture's edge? The afternoon,

the evening, its first star; the morning.

Whenever we noticed her
standing in the stream, still
as a branch in dead air, we
would grab our binoculars,
watch her watching,
her eye fixed on the water
slowly making its own way
around stumps, over a boulder,
under some leaves matted against
a fallen log. She seemed
to appear, stand, peer, then
lift one leg, stretch it, let
a foot quietly settle into the mud
then pull up her other foot, settle
it, and stare again, each step
tendered, an ideogram at the end
of a calligrapher's brush.
Every time she arrived, we watched
until, as if she had suddenly heard
a call in the sky, she would bend
her knees, raise her wide wings,
and lift into the welcome grace
of the air, her legs extending
back behind her, wings rising
and falling elegant under the clouds.
For more than a week now
we have not seen her. We watch
the sky, hoping to catch her great
feathered cross moving above the trees.